VERSUS

APPLE vs MICROSOFT
THE BATTLE OF BIG TECH

KENNY ABDO

Fly!
An Imprint of Abdo Zoom
abdobooks.com

abdobooks.com

Published by Abdo Zoom, a division of ABDO, P.O. Box 398166, Minneapolis, Minnesota 55439. Copyright © 2023 by Abdo Consulting Group, Inc. International copyrights reserved in all countries. No part of this book may be reproduced in any form without written permission from the publisher. Fly!™ is a trademark and logo of Abdo Zoom.

Printed in China.
102022
012023

Photo Credits: Alamy, AP Images, Getty Images, Shutterstock,
©Joi Ito p.21/ CC BY 2.0
Production Contributors: Kenny Abdo, Jennie Forsberg, Grace Hansen
Design Contributors: Candice Keimig, Neil Klinepier, Laura Graphenteen

Library of Congress Control Number: 2021950284

Publisher's Cataloging-in-Publication Data

Names: Abdo, Kenny, author.
Title: Apple vs. Microsoft: the battle of big tech / by Kenny Abdo.
Other title: the battle of big tech
Description: Minneapolis, Minnesota : Abdo Zoom, 2023 | Series: Versus | Includes online resources and index.
Identifiers: ISBN 9781098228613 (lib. bdg.) | ISBN 9781098229450 (ebook) | ISBN 9781098229870 (Read-to-Me ebook)
Subjects: LCSH: Apple Inc.--Juvenile literature. | Microsoft Corporation--Juvenile literature. | Technology in popular culture--Juvenile literature. | Mass media and technology--Juvenile literature. | Competition--Economic aspects--Juvenile literature.
Classification: DDC 338.7--dc23

TABLE OF CONTENTS

Apple vs. Microsoft............. 4

The Companies................. 8

Fight!......................... 14

Legacy........................ 18

Glossary...................... 22

Online Resources 23

Index 24

APPLE vs MICROSOFT

Apple and Microsoft are two of the biggest companies in the world. But the battle for the top has lasted for decades.

For more than 30 years, owners Steve Jobs and Bill Gates had a rollercoaster of a relationship. From reluctant allies to resentful foes, they were finally able to become something like friends.

THE COMPANIES

Bill Gates and lifelong friend Paul Allen created Microsoft in 1975. The name combines the words "microcomputer" and "**software**," which the company focused on.

In 1976, Steve Jobs started the Apple Computer Company in his garage. Jobs, along with Steve Wozniak and Ronald Wayne, wanted to make state-of-the-art **desktop** computers.

Jobs and Gates were friendly and often helped each other out. But when Microsoft announced the release of its new product Windows, the relationship soured into a heated rivalry.

FIGHT!

Apple sued Microsoft in 1994 over copying certain tech advances. The high-profile case found that Microsoft did not violate Apple's **copyrights**.

In 1996, Jobs had some less-than-kind words for Gates: "The only problem with Microsoft is they just have no taste...they just make really third-rate products."

In 1997, Apple's **stock** price dropped greatly. Gates stepped in and helped keep Apple from going **bankrupt**. Jobs appeared on the cover of *TIME*, thanking Gates for saving his company.

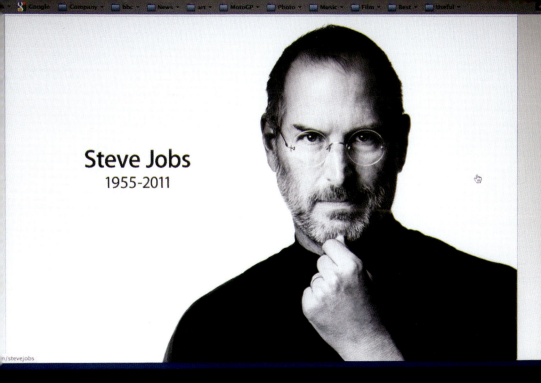

After Jobs passed away in 2011, Gates said, "I respect Steve, we got to work together. We spurred each other on, even as competitors."

LEGACY

Gates left Microsoft in 2008 to focus on his **charity** work. It remains one of the world's largest technology companies. In 2021 alone, Microsoft had more than 160 billion dollars in sales!

In 2015, Apple became the first ever $700 billion company. Shortly after, it overtook Google as the most valuable brand in the world. It continues to **innovate** and influence how people live to this day.

As of today, Apple still edges out Microsoft as one of the biggest companies in the world. However, as it was in the decades before, the two tech giants will continue to be neck and neck.

GLOSSARY

bankrupt – legally declared unable to pay something owed.

charity – a group or fund that helps people in need.

copyright – a law that gives the owner of a creative work the right to do whatever they want with it.

desktop – a computer that is setup and used on a desk.

innovate – to come up with a new idea, method, or device.

software – a program or instructions that tell a computer what to do.

stock – a share in the ownership of a fraction of a group or company.

ONLINE RESOURCES

To learn more about Apple and Microsoft, please visit **abdobooklinks.com** or scan this QR code. These links are routinely monitored and updated to provide the most current information available.

INDEX

Allen, Paul 9

Gates, Bill 6, 9, 13, 15, 16, 17, 18

Google 20

Jobs, Steve 6, 10, 13, 15, 16, 17

lawsuits 14

TIME (magazine) 16

Wayne, Ronald 10

Wozniak, Steve 10